THE PRINCIPLES OF COMMUNISM

FRIEDRICH ENGELS

SANAGE
PUBLISHING HOUSE

Paperback: 978-939089641-7

Sanage Publishing House LLP
Mumbai, India

sanagepublishing@gmail.com

Friedrich Engels, sometimes anglicised as **Frederick Engels** (28 November 1820 – 5 August 1895), was a German philosopher, economist, historian, political theorist and revolutionary socialist.

Engels developed what is now known as Marxism together with Karl Marx. In 1848, Engels co-authored *The Communist Manifesto* with Marx and also authored and co-authored (primarily with Marx) many other works.

CONTENTS

HISTORIC CONTEXT

In 1847 Engels wrote two draft programmes for the Communist League in the form of a catechism, one in June and the other in October. The latter, which is known as *Principles of Communism*, was first published in 1914. The earlier document *Draft of the Communist Confession of Faith*, was only found in 1968. It was first published in 1969 in Hamburg, together with four other documents pertaining to the first congress of the Communist League, in a booklet entitled *Gründungs Dokumente des Bundes der Kommunisten (Juni bis September 1847)* (Founding Documents of the Communist League).

At the June 1847 Congress of the League of the Just, which was also the founding conference of the Communist League, it was decided to issue a draft "confession of faith" to be submitted for discussion to the sections of the League. The document which has now come to light is almost certainly this draft. Comparison of the two documents shows that *Principles of Communism* is a revised edition of this earlier draft. In *Principles of Communism*, Engels left three questions unanswered, in two cases with the notation "unchanged" (bleibt); this clearly refers to the answers provided in the earlier draft.

The new draft for the programme was worked out by Engels

on the instructions of the leading body of the Paris circle of the Communist League. The instructions were decided on after Engles' sharp criticism at the committee meeting, on October 22, 1847, of the draft programme drawn up by the "true socialist" Moses Hess, which was then rejected.

Still considering Principles of Communism as a preliminary draft, Engels expressed the view, in a letter to Marx dated November 23-24 1847, that it would be best to drop the old catechistic form and draw up a programme in the form of a manifesto.

> "Think over the Confession of Faith a bit. I believe we had better drop the catechism form and call the thing: Communist Manifesto. As more or less history has got to be related in it, the form it has been in hitherto is quite unsuitable. I am bringing what I have done here with me; it is in simple narrative form, but miserably worded, in fearful haste. ..."

At the second congress of the Communist League (November 29-December 8, 1847) Marx and Engels defended the fundamental scientific principles of communism and were trusted with drafting a programme in the form of a manifesto of the Communist Party. In writing the manifesto the founders of Marxism made use of the propositions enunciated in Principles of Communism.

Engels uses the term *Manufaktur*, and its derivatives, which have been translated "manufacture", "manufacturing", etc., Engels used this word literally, to indicate production by hand, not factory production for which Engels uses "big industry". *Manufaktur* differs from handicraft (guild production in mediaeval towns), in that the latter was carried out by independent artisans. *Manufacktur* is carried out by homeworkers working for merchant capitalists, or by groups of craftspeople working together in large workshops owned by capitalists. It is therefore a transitional mode of production, between guild (handicraft) and modern (capitalist) forms of production.

o o o

THE PRINCIPLES OF COMMUNISM

ooo 1 ooo

WHAT IS COMMUNISM?

Communism is the doctrine of the conditions of the liberation of the proletariat.

ooo 2 ooo

WHAT IS THE PROLETARIAT?

The proletariat is that class in society which lives entirely from the sale of its labor and does not draw profit from any kind of capital; whose weal and woe, whose life and death, whose sole existence depends on the demand for labor – hence, on the changing state of business, on the vagaries of unbridled competition. The proletariat, or the class of proletarians, is, in a word, the working class of the 19th century.[1]

ooo 3 ooo

PROLETARIANS, THEN, HAVE NOT ALWAYS EXISTED?

No. There have always been poor and working classes; and the working class have mostly been poor. But there have not always been workers and poor people living under conditions as they are today; in other words, there have not always been proletarians, any more than there has always been free unbridled competitions.

○○○ 4 ○○○

HOW DID THE PROLETARIAT ORIGINATE?

The Proletariat originated in the industrial revolution, which took place in England in the last half of the last (18th) century, and which has since then been repeated in all the civilized countries of the world.

This industrial revolution was precipitated by the discovery of the steam engine, various spinning machines, the mechanical loom, and a whole series of other mechanical devices. These machines, which were very expensive and hence could be bought only by big capitalists, altered the whole mode of production and displaced the former workers, because the machines turned out cheaper and better commodities than the workers could produce with their inefficient spinning wheels and handlooms. The machines delivered industry wholly into the hands of the big capitalists and rendered entirely worthless the meagre property of the workers (tools, looms, etc.). The result was that the capitalists soon had everything in their hands and nothing remained to the workers. This marked the introduction of the factory system into the textile industry.

Once the impulse to the introduction of machinery and the factory system had been given, this system spread quickly to all other branches of industry, especially cloth- and book-printing, pottery, and the metal industries.

Labor was more and more divided among the individual workers so that the worker who previously had done a complete piece of work now did only a part of that piece. This division of labor made it possible to produce things faster and cheaper. It reduced the activity of the individual worker to simple, endlessly repeated mechanical motions which could be performed not only as well but much better by a machine. In this way, all these industries fell, one after another, under the dominance of steam, machinery, and the factory system, just as spinning and weaving had already done.

But at the same time, they also fell into the hands of big capitalists, and their workers were deprived of whatever independence remained to them. Gradually, not only genuine manufacture but also handicrafts came within the province of the factory system as big capitalists increasingly displaced the small master craftsmen by setting up huge workshops, which saved many expenses and permitted an elaborate division of labor.

This is how it has come about that in civilized countries at the present time nearly all kinds of labor are performed in factories – and, in nearly all branches of work, handicrafts and manufacture have been superseded. This process has, to an ever greater degree, ruined the old middle class, especially the small handicraftsmen; it has entirely transformed the condition of the workers; and two new classes have been created which are gradually swallowing up all the others. These are:

(i) The class of big capitalists, who, in all civilized countries, are already in almost exclusive possession of all the means of subsistance and of the instruments (machines, factories) and materials necessary for the production of the means of subsistence. This is the bourgeois class, or the bourgeoisie.

(ii) The class of the wholly propertyless, who are obliged to sell their labor to the bourgeoisie in order to get, in exchange, the means of subsistence for their support. This is called the class of proletarians, or the proletariat.

○ ○ ○ 5 ○ ○ ○

UNDER WHAT CONDITIONS DOES THIS SALE OF THE LABOR OF THE PROLETARIANS TO THE BOURGEOISIE TAKE PLACE?

Labor is a commodity, like any other, and its price is therefore determined by exactly the same laws that apply to other commodities. In a regime of big industry or of free competition – as we shall see, the two come to the same thing – the price of a commodity is, on the average, always equal to its cost of production. Hence, the price of labor is also equal to the cost of production of labor.

But, the costs of production of labor consist of precisely the quantity of means of subsistence necessary to enable the worker to continue working, and to prevent the working class from dying out. The worker will therefore get no more for his labor than is necessary for this purpose; the price of labor, or the wage, will, in other words, be the lowest, the minimum, required for the maintenance of life.

However, since business is sometimes better and sometimes worse, it follows that the worker sometimes gets more and sometimes gets less for his commodities. But, again, just as the industrialist, on the average of good times and bad, gets no more and no less for his commodities than what they cost, similarly on the average the worker gets no more and no less than his minimum.

This economic law of wages operates the more strictly the greater the degree to which big industry has taken possession of all branches of production.

○ ○ ○ **6** ○ ○ ○

WHAT WORKING CLASSES WERE THERE BEFORE THE INDUSTRIAL REVOLUTION?

The working classes have always, according to the different stages of development of society, lived in different circumstances and had different relations to the owning and ruling classes.

In antiquity, the workers were the slaves of the owners, just as they still are in many backward countries and even in the southern part of the United States.

In the Middle Ages, they were the serfs of the land-owning nobility, as they still are in Hungary, Poland, and Russia. In the Middle Ages, and indeed right up to the industrial revolution, there were also journeymen in the cities who worked in the service of petty bourgeois masters. Gradually, as manufacture developed, these journeymen became manufacturing workers who were even then employed by larger capitalists.

○ ○ ○ **7** ○ ○ ○

IN WHAT WAY DO PROLETARIANS DIFFER FROM SLAVES?

The slave is sold once and for all; the proletarian must sell himself daily and hourly.

The individual slave, property of one master, is assured an existence, however miserable it may be, because of the master's interest. The individual proletarian, property as it were of the entire bourgeois class which buys his labor only when someone has need of it, has no secure existence. This existence is assured only to the class as a whole.

The slave is outside competition; the proletarian is in it and experiences all its vagaries.

The slave counts as a thing, not as a member of society. Thus, the slave can have a better existence than the proletarian, while the proletarian belongs to a higher stage of social development and, himself, stands on a higher social level than the slave.

The slave frees himself when, of all the relations of private property, he abolishes only the relation of slavery and thereby becomes a proletarian; the proletarian can free himself only by abolishing private property in general.

○ ○ ○ **8** ○ ○ ○

IN WHAT WAY DO PROLETARIANS DIFFER FROM SERFS?

The serf possesses and uses an instrument of production, a piece of land, in exchange for which he gives up a part of his product or part of the services of his labor.

The proletarian works with the instruments of production of another, for the account of this other, in exchange for a part of the product.

The serf gives up, the proletarian receives. The serf has an assured existence, the proletarian has not. The serf is outside competition, the proletarian is in it.

The serf liberates himself in one of three ways: either he runs away to the city and there becomes a handicraftsman;

or, instead of products and services, he gives money to his lord and thereby becomes a free tenant; or he overthrows his feudal lord and himself becomes a property owner. In short, by one route or another, he gets into the owning class and enters into competition. The proletarian liberates himself by abolishing competition, private property, and all class differences.

○ ○ ○ **9** ○ ○ ○

IN WHAT WAY DO PROLETARIANS DIFFER FROM HANDICRAFTSMEN?

In contrast to the proletarian, the so-called handicraftsman, as he still existed almost everywhere in the past (eighteenth) century and still exists here and there at present, is a proletarian at most temporarily. His goal is to acquire capital himself wherewith to exploit other workers. He can often achieve this goal where guilds still exist or where freedom from guild restrictions has not yet led to the introduction of factory-style methods into the crafts nor yet to fierce competition But as soon as the factory system has been introduced into the crafts and competition flourishes fully, this perspective dwindles away and the handicraftsman becomes more and more a proletarian. The handicraftsman therefore frees himself by becoming either bourgeois or entering the middle class in general, or becoming a proletarian because of competition (as is now more often the case). In which case he can free himself by joining the proletarian movement, i.e., the more or less communist movement. [2]

∘ ∘ ∘ 10 ∘ ∘ ∘

IN WHAT WAY DO PROLETARIANS DIFFER FROM MANUFACTURING WORKERS?

The manufacturing worker of the 16th to the 18th centuries still had, with but few exception, an instrument of production in his own possession – his loom, the family spinning wheel, a little plot of land which he cultivated in his spare time. The proletarian has none of these things.

The manufacturing worker almost always lives in the countryside and in a more or less patriarchal relation to his landlord or employer; the proletarian lives, for the most part, in the city and his relation to his employer is purely a cash relation.

The manufacturing worker is torn out of his patriarchal relation by big industry, loses whatever property he still has, and in this way becomes a proletarian.

∘ ∘ ∘ 11 ∘ ∘ ∘

WHAT WERE THE IMMEDIATE CONSEQUENCES OF THE INDUSTRIAL REVOLUTION AND OF THE DIVISION OF SOCIETY INTO BOURGEOISIE AND PROLETARIAT?

First, the lower and lower prices of industrial products brought about by machine labor totally destroyed, in all countries of the world, the old system of manufacture or industry based upon hand labor.

In this way, all semi-barbarian countries, which had hitherto been more or less strangers to historical development, and whose industry had been based on manufacture, were violently forced out of their isolation. They bought the cheaper commodities of the English and allowed their own manufacturing workers to be ruined. Countries which had known no progress for thousands of years – for example, India – were thoroughly revolutionized, and even China is now on the way to a revolution.

We have come to the point where a new machine invented in England deprives millions of Chinese workers of their livelihood within a year's time.

In this way, big industry has brought all the people of the Earth into contact with each other, has merged all local markets into one world market, has spread civilization and progress everywhere and has thus ensured that whatever happens in civilized countries will have repercussions in all other countries.

It follows that if the workers in England or France now liberate themselves, this must set off revolution in all other countries – revolutions which, sooner or later, must accomplish the liberation of their respective working class.

Second, wherever big industries displaced manufacture, the bourgeoisie developed in wealth and power to the utmost and made itself the first class of the country. The result was that wherever this happened, the bourgeoisie took political power into its own hands and displaced the hitherto ruling classes, the aristocracy, the guildmasters, and their representative, the absolute monarchy.

The bourgeoisie annihilated the power of the aristocracy, the nobility, by abolishing the entailment of estates – in other words, by making landed property subject to purchase and sale, and by doing away with the special privileges of the nobility. It destroyed the power of the guildmasters by abolishing guilds and handicraft privileges. In their place, it put competition – that is, a state of society in which everyone has the right to enter into any branch of industry, the only obstacle being a lack of the necessary capital.

The introduction of free competition is thus public declaration that from now on the members of society are unequal only to the extent that their capitals are unequal, that capital is the decisive power, and that therefore the capitalists, the bourgeoisie, have become the first class in society.

Free competition is necessary for the establishment of big industry, because it is the only condition of society in which big industry can make its way.

Having destroyed the social power of the nobility and the guildmasters, the bourgeois also destroyed their political power. Having raised itself to the actual position of first class in society, it proclaims itself to be also the dominant political class. This it does through the introduction of the representative system which rests on bourgeois equality before the law and the recognition of free competition, and in European countries takes the form of constitutional monarchy. In these constitutional monarchies, only those who possess a certain capital are voters – that is to say, only members of the bourgeoisie. These bourgeois voters choose the deputies, and these bourgeois deputies, by using their right to refuse to vote taxes, choose a bourgeois government.

Third, everywhere the proletariat develops in step with the bourgeoisie. In proportion, as the bourgeoisie grows in wealth, the proletariat grows in numbers. For, since the proletarians can be employed only by capital, and since capital extends only through employing labor, it follows that the growth of the proletariat proceeds at precisely the same pace as the growth of capital.

Simultaneously, this process draws members of the bourgeoisie and proletarians together into the great cities where industry can be carried on most profitably, and by thus throwing great masses in one spot it gives to the proletarians a consciousness of their own strength.

Moreover, the further this process advances, the more new labor-saving machines are invented, the greater is the pressure exercised by big industry on wages, which, as we have seen, sink to their minimum and therewith render the condition of the proletariat increasingly unbearable. The growing dissatisfaction of the proletariat thus joins with its rising power to prepare a proletarian social revolution.

○○○ 12 ○○○

WHAT WERE THE FURTHER CONSEQUENCES OF THE INDUSTRIAL REVOLUTION?

Big industry created in the steam engine, and other machines, the means of endlessly expanding industrial production, speeding it up, and cutting its costs. With production thus facilitated, the free competition, which is necessarily bound up with big industry, assumed the most extreme forms; a multitude of capitalists invaded industry, and, in a short while, more was produced than was needed.

As a consequence, finished commodities could not be sold, and a so-called commercial crisis broke out. Factories had to be closed, their owners went bankrupt, and the workers were without bread. Deepest misery reigned everywhere.

After a time, the superfluous products were sold, the factories began to operate again, wages rose, and gradually business got better than ever.

But it was not long before too many commodities were again produced and a new crisis broke out, only to follow the same course as its predecessor.

Ever since the beginning of this (19th) century, the condition of industry has constantly fluctuated between periods of prosperity and periods of crisis; nearly every five to seven years, a fresh crisis has intervened, always with the greatest hardship for workers, and always accompanied by general revolutionary stirrings and the direct peril to the whole existing order of things.

○ ○ ○ 13 ○ ○ ○

WHAT FOLLOWS FROM THESE PERIODIC COMMERCIAL CRISES?

First:

That, though big industry in its earliest stage created free competition, it has now outgrown free competition;

that, for big industry, competition and generally the individualistic organization of production have become a fetter which it must and will shatter;

that, so long as big industry remains on its present footing, it can be maintained only at the cost of general chaos every seven years, each time threatening the whole of civilization and not only plunging the proletarians into misery but also ruining large sections of the bourgeoisie;

hence, either that big industry must itself be given up, which is an absolute impossibility, or that it makes unavoidably necessary an entirely new organization of society in which production is no longer directed by mutually competing individual industrialists but rather by the whole society operating according to a definite plan and taking account of the needs of all.

Second: That big industry, and the limitless expansion of production which it makes possible, bring within the range of feasibility a social order in which so much is produced that every member of society will be in a position to exercise and develop all his powers and faculties in complete freedom.

It thus appears that the very qualities of big industry which, in our present-day society, produce misery and crises are those which, in a different form of society, will abolish this misery and these catastrophic depressions.

We see with the greatest clarity:

(i) That all these evils are from now on to be ascribed solely to a social order which no longer corresponds to the requirements of the real situation; and

(ii) That it is possible, through a new social order, to do away with these evils altogether.

○○○ 14 ○○○

WHAT WILL THIS NEW SOCIAL ORDER HAVE TO BE LIKE?

Above all, it will have to take the control of industry and of all branches of production out of the hands of mutually competing individuals, and instead institute a system in which all these branches of production are operated by society as a whole – that is, for the common account, according to a common plan, and with the participation of all members of society.

It will, in other words, abolish competition and replace it with association.

Moreover, since the management of industry by individuals necessarily implies private property, and since competition is in reality merely the manner and form in which the control of industry by private property owners expresses itself, it follows that private property cannot be separated from competition and the individual management of industry. Private property must, therefore, be abolished and in its place must come the common utilization of all instruments of production and the distribution of all products according to common agreement – in a word, what is called the communal ownership of goods.

In fact, the abolition of private property is, doubtless, the shortest and most significant way to characterize the revolution in the whole social order which has been made necessary by the development of industry – and for this reason it is rightly advanced by communists as their main demand.

○○○ 15 ○○○

WAS NOT THE ABOLITION OF PRIVATE PROPERTY POSSIBLE AT AN EARLIER TIME?

No. Every change in the social order, every revolution in property relations, is the necessary consequence of the creation of new forces of production which no longer fit into the old property relations.

Private property has not always existed.

When, towards the end of the Middle Ages, there arose a new mode of production which could not be carried on under the then existing feudal and guild forms of property, this manufacture, which had outgrown the old property relations, created a new property form, private property. And for manufacture and the earliest stage of development of big industry, private property was the only possible property form; the social order based on it was the only possible social order.

So long as it is not possible to produce so much that there is enough for all, with more left over for expanding the social capital and extending the forces of production – so long as this is not possible, there must always be a ruling class directing the use of society's productive forces, and a poor, oppressed class. How these classes are constituted depends on the stage of development.

The agrarian Middle Ages give us the baron and the serf; the cities of the later Middle Ages show us the guildmaster and the journeyman and the day laborer; the 17th century has its manufacturing workers; the 19th has big factory owners and proletarians.

It is clear that, up to now, the forces of production have never been developed to the point where enough could be developed for all, and that private property has become a fetter and a barrier in relation to the further development of the forces of production.

Now, however, the development of big industry has ushered in a new period. Capital and the forces of production have been expanded to an unprecedented extent, and the means are at hand to multiply them without limit in the near future. Moreover, the forces of production have been concentrated in the hands of a few bourgeois, while the great mass of the people are more and more falling into the proletariat, their situation becoming more wretched and intolerable in proportion to the increase of wealth of the bourgeoisie. And finally, these mighty and easily extended forces of production have so far outgrown private property and the bourgeoisie, that they threaten at any moment to unleash the most violent disturbances of the social order. Now, under these conditions, the abolition of private property has become not only possible but absolutely necessary.

○○○ 16 ○○○

WILL THE PEACEFUL ABOLITION OF PRIVATE PROPERTY BE POSSIBLE?

It would be desirable if this could happen, and the communists would certainly be the last to oppose it. Communists know only too well that all conspiracies are not only useless, but even harmful. They know all too well that revolutions are not made intentionally and arbitrarily, but that, everywhere and always, they have been the necessary consequence of conditions which were wholly independent of the will and direction of individual parties and entire classes.

But they also see that the development of the proletariat in nearly all civilized countries has been violently suppressed, and that in this way the opponents of communism have been working toward a revolution with all their strength. If the oppressed proletariat is finally driven to revolution, then we communists will defend the interests of the proletarians with deeds as we now defend them with words.

○○○ 17 ○○○

WILL IT BE POSSIBLE FOR PRIVATE PROPERTY TO BE ABOLISHED AT ONE STROKE?

No, no more than existing forces of production can at one stroke be multiplied to the extent necessary for the creation of a communal society.

In all probability, the proletarian revolution will transform existing society gradually and will be able to abolish private property only when the means of production are available in sufficient quantity.

○○○ 18 ○○○

WHAT WILL BE THE COURSE OF THIS REVOLUTION?

Above all, it will establish a democratic constitution, and through this, the direct or indirect dominance of the proletariat. Direct in England, where the proletarians are already a majority of the people. Indirect in France and Germany, where the majority of the people consists not only of proletarians, but also of small peasants and petty bourgeois who are in the process of falling into the proletariat, who are more and more dependent in all their political interests on the proletariat, and who must, therefore, soon adapt to the demands of the proletariat. Perhaps this will cost a second struggle, but the outcome can only be the victory of the proletariat.

Democracy would be wholly valueless to the proletariat if it were not immediately used as a means for putting through measures directed against private property and ensuring the livelihood of the proletariat. The main measures, emerging as the necessary result of existing relations, are the following:

(i) Limitation of private property through progressive taxation, heavy inheritance taxes, abolition of inheritance through collateral lines (brothers, nephews, etc.) forced loans, etc.

(ii) Gradual expropriation of landowners, industrialists, railroad magnates and shipowners, partly through competition by state industry, partly directly through compensation in the form of bonds.

(iii) Confiscation of the possessions of all emigrants and rebels against the majority of the people.

(iv) Organization of labor or employment of proletarians on publicly owned land, in factories and workshops, with competition among the workers being abolished and with the factory owners, in so far as they still exist, being obliged to pay the same high wages as those paid by the state.

(v) An equal obligation on all members of society to work until such time as private property has been completely abolished. Formation of industrial armies, especially for agriculture.

(vi) Centralization of money and credit in the hands of the state through a national bank with state capital, and the suppression of all private banks and bankers.

(vii) Increase in the number of national factories, workshops, railroads, ships; bringing new lands into cultivation and improvement of land already under cultivation – all in proportion to the growth of the capital and labor force at the disposal of the nation.

(viii) Education of all children, from the moment they can leave their mother's care, in national establishments at national cost. Education and production together.

(ix) Construction, on public lands, of great palaces as communal dwellings for associated groups of citizens engaged in both industry and agriculture and combining in their way of life the advantages of urban and rural conditions while avoiding the one-sidedness and drawbacks of each.

(x) Destruction of all unhealthy and jerry-built dwellings in urban districts.

(xi) Equal inheritance rights for children born in and out of wedlock.

(xii) Concentration of all means of transportation in the hands of the nation.

It is impossible, of course, to carry out all these measures at once. But one will always bring others in its wake. Once the first radical attack on private property has been launched, the proletariat will find itself forced to go ever further, to concentrate increasingly in the hands of the state all capital, all agriculture, all transport, all trade. All the foregoing measures are directed to this end; and they will become practicable and feasible, capable of producing their centralizing effects to precisely the degree that the proletariat, through its labor, multiplies the country's productive forces.

Finally, when all capital, all production, all exchange have been brought together in the hands of the nation, private property will disappear of its own accord, money will become superfluous, and production will so expand and man so change that society will be able to slough off whatever of its old economic habits may remain.

○ ○ ○ 19 ○ ○ ○

WILL IT BE POSSIBLE FOR THIS REVOLUTION TO TAKE PLACE IN ONE COUNTRY ALONE?

No. By creating the world market, big industry has already brought all the peoples of the Earth, and especially the civilized peoples, into such close relation with one another that none is independent of what happens to the others.

Further, it has co-ordinated the social development of the civilized countries to such an extent that, in all of them, bourgeoisie and proletariat have become the decisive classes, and the struggle between them the great struggle of the day. It follows that the communist revolution will not merely be a national phenomenon but must take place simultaneously in all civilized countries – that is to say, at least in England, America, France, and Germany.

It will develop in each of these countries more or less rapidly, according as one country or the other has a more developed industry, greater wealth, a more significant mass of productive forces. Hence, it will go slowest and will meet most obstacles in Germany, most rapidly and with the fewest difficulties in England. It will have a powerful impact on the other countries of the world, and will radically alter the course of development which they have followed up to now, while greatly stepping up its pace.

It is a universal revolution and will, accordingly, have a universal range.

○○○ 20 ○○○

WHAT WILL BE THE CONSEQUENCES OF THE ULTIMATE DISAPPEARANCE OF PRIVATE PROPERTY?

Society will take all forces of production and means of commerce, as well as the exchange and distribution of products, out of the hands of private capitalists and will manage them in accordance with a plan based on the availability of resources and the needs of the whole society. In this way, most important of all, the evil consequences which are now associated with the conduct of big industry will be abolished.

There will be no more crises; the expanded production, which for the present order of society is overproduction and hence a prevailing cause of misery, will then be insufficient and in need of being expanded much further. Instead of generating misery, overproduction will reach beyond the elementary requirements of society to assure the satisfaction of the needs of all; it will create new needs and, at the same time, the means of satisfying them. It will become the condition of, and the stimulus to, new progress, which will no longer throw the whole social order into confusion, as progress has always done in the past. Big industry, freed from the pressure of private property, will undergo such an expansion that what we now see will seem as petty in comparison as manufacture seems when put beside the big industry of our own day. This development of industry will make available to society a sufficient mass of products to satisfy the needs of everyone.

The same will be true of agriculture, which also suffers from the pressure of private property and is held back by the division of privately owned land into small parcels. Here, existing improvements and scientific procedures will be put into practice, with a resulting leap forward which will assure to society all the products it needs.

In this way, such an abundance of goods will be able to satisfy the needs of all its members.

The division of society into different, mutually hostile classes will then become unnecessary. Indeed, it will be not only unnecessary but intolerable in the new social order. The existence of classes originated in the division of labor, and the division of labor, as it has been known up to the present, will completely disappear. For mechanical and chemical processes are not enough to bring industrial and agricultural production up to the level we have described; the capacities of the men who make use of these processes must undergo a corresponding development.

Just as the peasants and manufacturing workers of the last century changed their whole way of life and became quite different people when they were drawn into big industry, in the same way, communal control over production by society as a whole, and the resulting new development, will both require an entirely different kind of human material.

People will no longer be, as they are today, subordinated to a single branch of production, bound to it, exploited by it; they will no longer develop one of their faculties at the expense of all others; they will no longer know only one branch, or one branch of a single branch, of production as a whole. Even industry as it is today is finding such people less and less useful.

Industry controlled by society as a whole, and operated according to a plan, presupposes well-rounded human beings, their faculties developed in balanced fashion, able to see the system of production in its entirety.

The form of the division of labor which makes one a peasant, another a cobbler, a third a factory worker, a fourth a stock-market operator, has already been undermined by machinery and will completely disappear. Education will enable young people quickly to familiarize themselves with the whole system of production and to pass from one branch of production to another in response to the needs of society or their own inclinations. It will, therefore, free them from the one-sided character which the present-day division of labor impresses upon every individual. Communist society will, in this way, make it possible for its members to put their comprehensively developed faculties to full use. But, when this happens, classes will necessarily disappear. It follows that society organized on a communist basis is incompatible with the existence of classes on the one hand, and that the very building of such a society provides the means of abolishing class differences on the other.

A corollary of this is that the difference between city and country is destined to disappear. The management of agriculture and industry by the same people rather than by two different classes of people is, if only for purely material reasons, a necessary condition of communist association. The dispersal of the agricultural population on the land, alongside the crowding of the industrial population into the great cities, is a condition which corresponds to an undeveloped state of both agriculture and industry and can already be felt as an obstacle to further development.

The general co-operation of all members of society for the purpose of planned exploitation of the forces of production, the expansion of production to the point where it will satisfy the needs of all, the abolition of a situation in which the needs of some are satisfied at the expense of the needs of others, the complete liquidation of classes and their conflicts, the rounded development of the capacities of all members of society through the elimination of the present division of labor, through industrial education, through engaging in varying activities, through the participation by all in the enjoyments produced by all, through the combination of city and country – these are the main consequences of the abolition of private property.

○ ○ ○ 21 ○ ○ ○

WHAT WILL BE THE INFLUENCE OF COMMUNIST SOCIETY ON THE FAMILY?

It will transform the relations between the sexes into a purely private matter which concerns only the persons involved and into which society has no occasion to intervene. It can do this since it does away with private property and educates children on a communal basis, and in this way removes the two bases of traditional marriage – the dependence rooted in private property, of the women on the man, and of the children on the parents.

And here is the answer to the outcry of the highly moral philistines against the “community of women”. Community of women is a condition which belongs entirely to bourgeois society and which today finds its complete expression in prostitution. But prostitution is based on private property and falls with it. Thus, communist society, instead of introducing community of women, in fact abolishes it.

○ ○ ○ 22 ○ ○ ○

WHAT WILL BE THE ATTITUDE OF COMMUNISM TO EXISTING NATIONALITIES?

The nationalities of the peoples associating themselves in accordance with the principle of community will be compelled to mingle with each other as a result of this association and thereby to dissolve themselves, just as the various estate and class distinctions must disappear through the abolition of their basis, private property.[3]

○ ○ ○ 23 ○ ○ ○

WHAT WILL BE ITS ATTITUDE TO EXISTING RELIGIONS?

All religions so far have been the expression of historical stages of development of individual peoples or groups of peoples. But communism is the stage of historical development which makes all existing religions superfluous and brings about their disappearance[4].

○ ○ ○ 24 ○ ○ ○

HOW DO COMMUNISTS DIFFER FROM SOCIALISTS?

The so-called socialists are divided into three categories.

[REACTIONARY SOCIALISTS:]

The first category consists of adherents of a feudal and

patriarchal society which has already been destroyed, and is still daily being destroyed, by big industry and world trade and their creation, bourgeois society. This category concludes, from the evils of existing society, that feudal and patriarchal society must be restored because it was free of such evils. In one way or another, all their proposals are directed to this end.

This category of reactionary socialists, for all their seeming partisanship and their scalding tears for the misery of the proletariat, is nevertheless energetically opposed by the communists for the following reasons:

(i) It strives for something which is entirely impossible.

(ii) It seeks to establish the rule of the aristocracy, the guildmasters, the small producers, and their retinue of absolute or feudal monarchs, officials, soldiers, and priests – a society which was, to be sure, free of the evils of present-day society but which brought it at least as many evils without even offering to the oppressed workers the prospect of liberation through a communist revolution.

(iii) As soon as the proletariat becomes revolutionary and communist, these reactionary socialists show their true colors by immediately making common cause with the bourgeoisie against the proletarians.

[BOURGEOIS SOCIALISTS:]

The second category consists of adherents of present-day society who have been frightened for its future by the evils to which it necessarily gives rise. What they want, therefore, is to maintain this society while getting rid of the evils which are an inherent part of it.

To this end, some propose mere welfare measures – while others come forward with grandiose systems of reform which, under the pretense of re-organizing society, are in fact intended to preserve the foundations, and hence the life, of existing society.

Communists must unremittingly struggle against these bourgeois socialists because they work for the enemies of communists and protect the society which communists aim to overthrow.

[DEMOCRATIC SOCIALISTS:]

Finally, the third category consists of democratic socialists who favor some of the same measures the communists advocate, as described in Question 18, not as part of the transition to communism, however, but as measures which they believe will be sufficient to abolish the misery and evils of present-day society.

These democratic socialists are either proletarians who are not yet sufficiently clear about the conditions of the liberation of their class, or they are representatives of the petty bourgeoisie, a class which, prior to the achievement of democracy and the socialist measures to which it gives rise, has many interests in common with the proletariat.

It follows that, in moments of action, the communists will have to come to an understanding with these democratic socialists, and in general to follow as far as possible a common policy with them – provided that these socialists do not enter into the service of the ruling bourgeoisie and attack the communists.

It is clear that this form of co-operation in action does not exclude the discussion of differences.

○ ○ ○ 25 ○ ○ ○

WHAT IS THE ATTITUDE OF THE COMMUNISTS TO THE OTHER POLITICAL PARTIES OF OUR TIME?

This attitude is different in the different countries.

In England, France, and Belgium, where the bourgeoisie rules, the communists still have a common interest with the various democratic parties, an interest which is all the greater the more closely the socialistic measures they champion approach the aims of the communists – that is, the more clearly and definitely they represent the interests of the proletariat and the more they depend on the proletariat for support. In England, for example, the working-class Chartists are infinitely closer to the communists than the democratic petty bourgeoisie or the so-called Radicals.

In America, where a democratic constitution has already been established, the communists must make the common cause with the party which will turn this constitution against the bourgeoisie and use it in the interests of the proletariat – that is, with the agrarian National Reformers.

In Switzerland, the Radicals, though a very mixed party, are the only group with which the communists can co-operate, and, among these Radicals, the Vaudois and Genevese are the most advanced.

In Germany, finally, the decisive struggle now on the order of the day is that between the bourgeoisie and the absolute monarchy. Since the communists cannot enter upon the decisive struggle between themselves and the bourgeoisie until the bourgeoisie is in power, it follows that it is in the interest of the communists to help the bourgeoisie to power as soon as possible in order the sooner to be able to overthrow it. Against the governments, therefore, the communists must continually support the radical liberal party, taking care to avoid the self-deceptions of the bourgeoisie and not fall for the enticing promises of benefits which a victory for the bourgeoisie would allegedly bring to the proletariat. The sole advantages which the proletariat would derive from a bourgeois victory would consist

(i) in various concessions which would facilitate the unification of the proletariat into a closely knit, battle-worthy, and organized class; and

(ii) in the certainly that, on the very day the absolute monarchies fall, the struggle between bourgeoisie and proletariat will start. From that day on, the policy of the communists will be the same as it now is in the countries where the bourgeoisie is already in power.

o o o

1. In their works written in later periods, Marx and Engels substituted the more accurate concepts of "sale of labour power", "value of labour power" and "price of labour power" (first introduced by Marx) for "sale of labour", "value of labour" and "price of labour", as used here.

2. Engels left half a page blank here in the manuscript. The *Draft of the Communist Confession of Faith*, has the answer shown for the same question (Number 12).

3. Engels' put "unchanged" here, referring to the answer in the June draft under No. 21 which is shown.

4. Similarly, this refers to the answer to Question 23 in the June draft.

5. The Chartists were the participants in the political movement of the British workers which lasted from the 1830s to the middle 1850s and had as its slogan the adoption of a People's Charter, demanding universal franchise and a series of conditions guaranteeing voting rights for all workers. Lenin defined Chartism as the world's "first broad, truly mass and politically organized proletarian revolutionary movement" (Collected Works, Eng. ed., Progress Publishers, Moscow, 1965, Vol. 29, p. 309.) The decline of the Chartist movement was due to the strengthening of Britain's industrial and commercial monopoly and the bribing of the upper stratum of the working class ("the labour aristocracy") by the British bourgeoisie out of its super-profits. Both factors led to the strengthening of opportunist tendencies in this stratum as expressed, in particular, by the refusal of the trade union leaders to support Chartism.

6. Probably a references to the National Reform Association, founded during the 1840s by George H. Evans, with headquarters in New York City, which had for its motto, "Vote Yourself a Farm".